VOICES · IN · POETRY

EDGAR ALLAN POE

TEXT BY
AARON FRISCH

ILLUSTRATIONS BY
GARY KELLEY

WITH SELECTED PHOTOS BY TINA MUCCI

CREATIVE EDUCATION

*G*aily bedight,

A gallant knight,

In sunshine and in shadow,

Had journeyed long,

Singing a song,

In search of Eldorado.

But he grew old—

This knight so bold—

And o'er his heart a shadow

Fell, as he found

No spot of ground

That looked like Eldorado.

And, as his strength

Failed him at length,

He met a pilgrim shadow—

'Shadow,' said he,

'Where can it be—

This land of Eldorado?'

'Over the Mountains

Of the Moon,

Down the Valley of the Shadow,

Ride, boldly ride,'

The shade replied,—

'If you seek for Eldorado!'

From *The Works of the Late Edgar Allan Poe*

INTRODUCTION

*H*e never really found his place. Orphaned at two and never adopted, he spent his adult life roaming from city to city and job to job, facing poverty, addiction, and death at every turn. His efforts with a pen were mostly sneered at and dismissed. Even his face—with its expansive forehead and dark eyes—was not one to blend into a crowd. And always pursuing him were the voices that whispered in his ear, telling him he was going insane.

Perhaps no poet endured a life so hard as that of Edgar Allan Poe. His was a lonely existence of little fame and even less fortune. "It was my crime to have no one on Earth who cared for me, or loved me," he once said. Still he labored on, forging a most unique literary legacy under these heavy burdens of fate. He threw open doors to shadowed beauty and windows onto the soul, yet it wasn't until he took his final rest that the world at last found a place for this dark poet.

From childhood's hour I have not been

As others were—I have not seen

As others saw—I could not bring

My passions from a common spring—

From the same source I have not taken

My sorrow—I could not awaken

My heart to joy at the same tone—

And all I lov'd—*I* lov'd alone—

Then—in my childhood—in the dawn

Of a most stormy life—was drawn

From ev'ry depth of good and ill

The mystery which binds me still—

From the torrent, or the fountain—

From the red cliff of the mountain—

From the sun that 'round me roll'd

In its autumn tint of gold—

From the lightning in the sky

As it pass'd me flying by—

From the thunder, and the storm—

And the cloud that took the form

(When the rest of Heaven was blue)

Of a demon in my view—

From *Collected Works of Edgar Allan Poe*

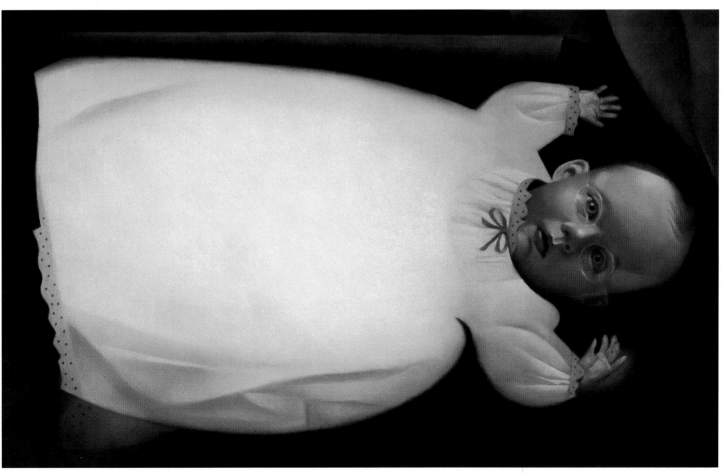

ORPHANED

Edgar Poe came into the world on January 19, 1809, in Boston, Massachusetts, where his parents—traveling actors Elizabeth Arnold and David Poe Jr.—were performing Shakespeare's *Hamlet* with a theater company. Edgar would never know them. Before he was two years old, his father abandoned the family and would soon die. Elizabeth continued her theater travels with Edgar and his four-year-old brother, Henry, in tow but developed tuberculosis. Soon after giving birth to a daughter named Rosalie, she died at age 24 in Richmond, Virginia.

The orphaned Poe children were split up. Henry was sent to live with his father's relatives in Baltimore, Maryland, while Edgar and Rosalie stayed in Richmond, each going to a different foster home. Edgar seemed fortunate to find himself under the roof of a childless, middle-class tobacco merchant named John Allan and his wife, Frances.

Edgar's first years in the Allan household were happy ones, and he was soon calling Frances "Ma." Frances and a sister living with the couple doted on Edgar, who grew into a bright and mischievous youngster. John was a stern man, but even he could not suppress a smile as Edgar marched around singing songs or danced on the dining room table in his stocking feet, grinning as the ladies applauded.

In 1815, the Allan family sailed to England on an extended business trip. Six-year-old Edgar was placed in Manor House School near London to begin his education. The school was surrounded by an iron-studded fence and gloomy elms, and the windows of its long, antiquated buildings let in a musty light. To reach his room, Edgar had to pass through a maze of narrow halls and dark stairwells. The foreboding atmosphere etched itself into the boy's imagination.

A 19th-century English boarding school

THE LAKE

*I*n spring of youth it was my lot

To haunt of the wide world a spot

The which I could not love the less—

So lovely was the loneliness

Of a wild lake, with black rock bound,

And the tall pines that towered around.

But when the Night had thrown her pall

Upon that spot, as upon all,

And the mystic wind went by

Murmuring in melody—

Then—ah then I would awake

To the terror of the lone lake.

Yet that terror was not fright,

But a tremulous delight—

A feeling not the jewelled mine

Could teach or bribe me to define—

Nor love—although the Love were thine.

Death was in that poisonous wave,

And in its gulf a fitting grave

For him who thence could solace bring

To his lone imagining—

Whose solitary soul could make

An Eden of that dim lake.

From *Tamerlane and Other Poems*

*I*n 1820, the Allans returned to Richmond, where Edgar continued his education. His early teenage years were typical ones, filled with school and sports. In the classroom, he showed a quick mind and sharp tongue and got good grades with little effort. Outside of class, he developed a wiry physique by running, boxing, or swimming for miles in the James River.

During his years in England, Edgar had felt like an outsider with his American accent. The feeling now lingered in the States as he looked upon classmates who had grown up together. It had also become known that he was born to actors—a disreputable profession in those days—and had never been formally adopted by the Allans, and some of the boys regarded him as inferior. "On looking back on it," one classmate later noted, "I fancy it gave him a fierceness he would otherwise not have had."

It was during these early teenage years that Edgar began writing poetry. As a young child, he had been enthralled with music, and his fertile mind loved the prospect of marrying music to his ideas and words. Many of his earliest efforts dealt with themes of love, and classical and religious lore. His first poems, including "O, Tempora! O, Mores!"

and "The Lake," were begun when he was as young as 14.

When he was 15, Edgar developed a crush on Jane Stanard, the mother of a classmate. Jane gave Edgar a kind attentiveness, and he called her Helen, the name that meant "beauty" in classical literature. Edgar was devastated when she fell ill and died in April 1824. Her death by tuberculosis mirrored that of Edgar's young mother, and the theme of a beautiful dying woman would stay with him. Years later, he would memorialize Jane in a poem entitled "To Helen."

When his grief passed, Edgar found a new love: a neighbor girl named Elmira Royster, to whom he was soon engaged. "Edgar was a beautiful boy," Elmira later said.

"He was not very talkative, and his general manner was sad, but when he did talk, his conversation was very pleasant. Edgar was warm and zealous in any cause he was interested in, being enthusiastic and impulsive. He had strong prejudices and hated everything coarse and unrefined."

As Edgar found love, he also found problems at home. He worshipped his foster mother, Frances, but was increasingly at odds with John, who seemed to expect a great deal of humility and gratitude from his foster child. Their feud escalated dramatically in 1824 when Edgar discovered that John was having an extramarital affair, and soon the two could barely stand to remain in the same room together.

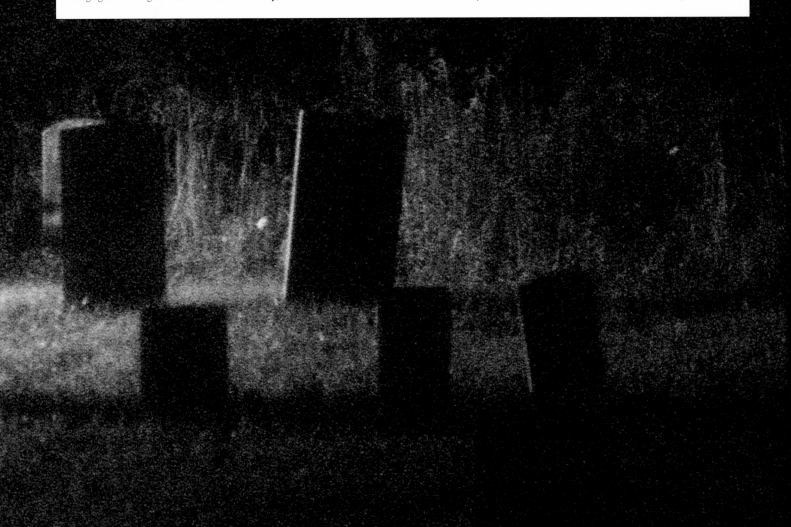

TO HELEN

*H*elen, thy beauty is to me

    Like those Nicéan barks of yore,

That gently, o'er a perfumed sea,

    The weary, way-worn wanderer bore

    To his own native shore.

On desperate seas long wont to roam,

    Thy hyacinth hair, thy classic face,

Thy Naiad airs have brought me home

    To the glory that was Greece,

    And the grandeur that was Rome.

Lo! in yon brilliant window-niche

    How statue-like I see thee stand,

The agate lamp within thy hand!

    Ah, Psyche, from the regions which

    Are Holy-Land!

From *Poems*

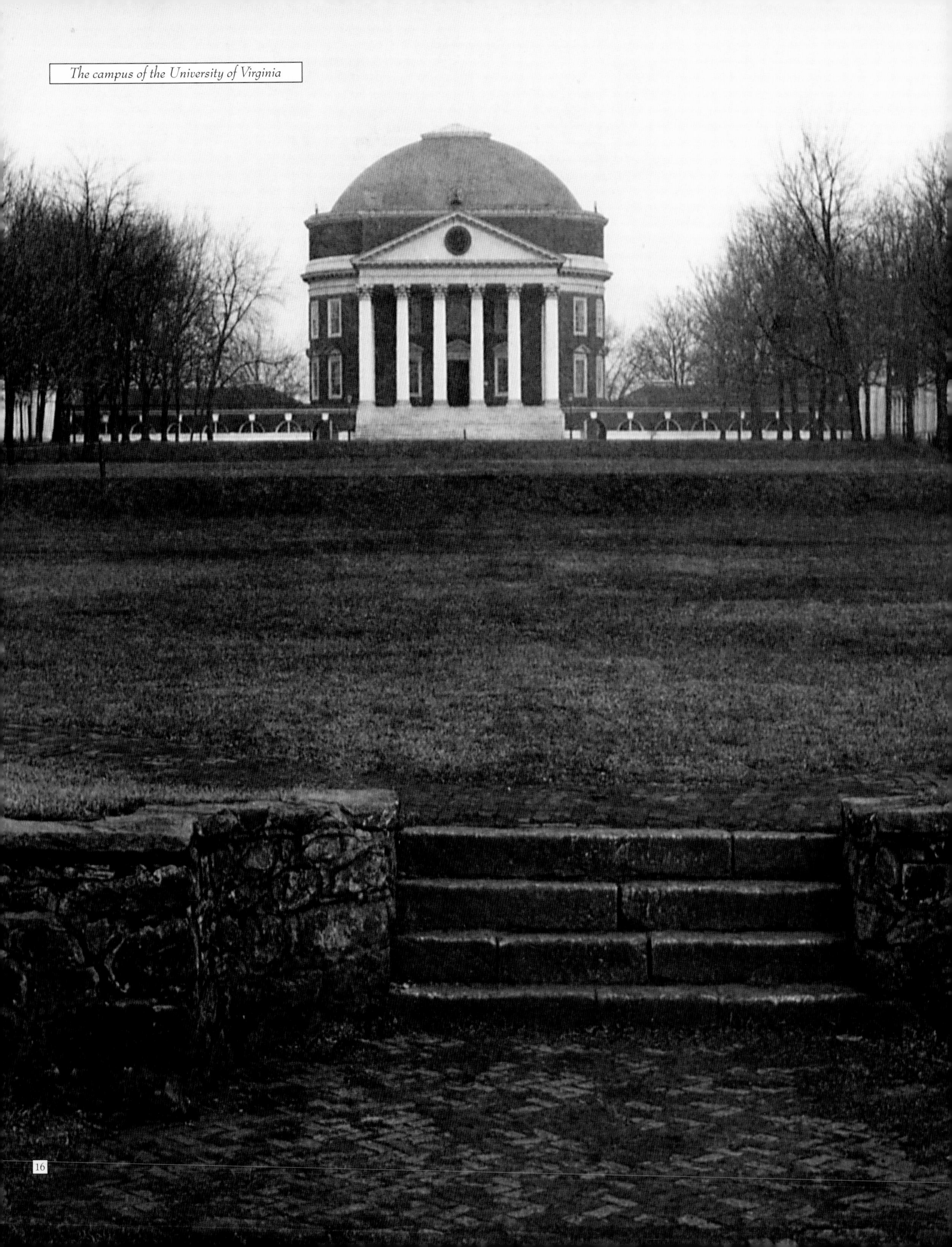

The campus of the University of Virginia

COLLEGE

*I*n 1826, Edgar Allan Poe left home for the elite University of Virginia. His foster father had inherited a small fortune from a wealthy uncle, and the Allan family was suddenly upper-class. As always, Poe proved an excellent student. Still, his mind was troubled. He had yet to receive a single letter from his fiancée, even though he had sent her many. It was months before he learned the distressing truth: Elmira's father had intercepted the letters, and she had at last given up on Poe and become engaged to another man.

Compounding Poe's heartbreak was his dire financial situation. John Allan had pushed him out the door almost penniless. As Poe's college mates—most the sons of wealthy southern planters—hired servants and indulged in fine clothes, Poe bought books on credit and dropped courses to make ends meet. He wrote his foster father many letters begging for money, but his pleas went unanswered.

Desperate, Poe threw himself into gambling, an illicit but popular activity at the university. As his losses piled up, he began drinking. By the end of his first term, Poe was more than $2,000 in debt (an amount equal to almost $40,000 today) and out of school. "He played in so impassioned a manner that it amounted almost to infatuation," a friend later recalled. "Card-playing and drinking alike were carried on under the spell of impulse or uncontrolled excitement."

His college hopes dashed, Poe went to Boston, where he tried acting and writing. His acting efforts were unsuccessful, but his work with a pen produced some promising results. In the summer of 1827, he anonymously published his first book, called *Tamerlane and Other Poems*. Only 40 copies were printed.

*K*ind solace in a dying hour!

Such, father, is not (now) my theme—

I will not madly deem that power

Of Earth may shrive me of the sin

Unearthly pride hath revell'd in—

I have no time to dote or dream:

You call it hope—that fire of fire!

It is but agony of desire:

If I *can* hope—Oh God! I can—

Its fount is holier—more divine—

I would not call thee fool, old man,

But such is not a gift of thine.

Know thou the secret of a spirit

Bow'd from its wild pride into shame.

O yearning heart! I did inherit

Thy withering portion with the fame,

The searing glory which hath shone

Amid the Jewels of my throne,

Halo of Hell! and with a pain

Not Hell shall make me fear again—

O craving heart, for the lost flowers

And sunshine of my summer hours!

The undying voice of that dead time,

With its interminable chime,

Rings, in the spirit of a spell,

Upon thy emptiness—a knell.

Excerpt from "Tamerlane," *Tamerlane and Other Poems*

MILITARY

By the time his first book was printed, Poe had enlisted in the United States Army. Although the army's strict atmosphere seemed an odd fit for an aspiring young writer, Poe adapted readily to the routine and rose to the rank of sergeant major within 18 months. And as the military paid his bills, Poe at last had no financial worries.

In February 1829, Frances Allan died of tuberculosis. On her deathbed, she pleaded with her husband to help Poe, and John reluctantly agreed to do so. Poe arrived in Richmond the day after the funeral, wracked with grief but hoping to mend fences with his foster father. John kept his word by helping Poe gain admission to prestigious West Point Academy, where he hoped to become a commissioned and better paid officer.

Despite his military aspirations, Poe still fancied himself a poet. In the year before he entered West Point, his second volume of poems, called *Al Aaraaf, Tamerlane and Minor Poems*, was published. In a letter to a potential publisher,

A view of West Point Academy, New York

Poe wrote, "I am young—not yet twenty—am a poet—if deep worship of all beauty can make me one—and wish to be so in the more common meaning of the word. I would give the world to embody one half the ideas afloat in my imagination."

Poe's time at West Point started well. Although it was said he never spent more than two minutes preparing for class, he received the usual excellent marks. He also was popular among his fellow cadets, largely because of the witty verses he penned ridiculing the academy's instructors. Reciting them behind closed doors, he left his companions rolling with laughter.

Yet despite his academic and social success, Poe was constantly anxious. John had remarried and resumed his tight-fisted ways, leaving Poe embarrassingly poor. As the months ticked by, the young cadet's illusions of a quick ascent to a comfortable military career also faded. Finally, in a calculated move, he ignored his classes and church and was dismissed from West Point. John then formally disowned him.

*L*o! Death has reared himself a throne
In a strange city lying alone
Far down within the dim West,
Where the good and the bad and the worst
    and the best
Have gone to their eternal rest.
There shrines and palaces and towers
(Time-eaten towers that tremble not!)
Resemble nothing that is ours.
Around, by lifting winds forgot,

Resignedly beneath the sky
The melancholy waters lie.

No rays from the holy heaven come down
On the long night-time of that town;
But light from out the lurid sea
Streams up the turrets silently—
Gleams up the pinnacles far and free—
Up domes—up spires—up kingly halls—
Up fanes—up Babylon-like walls—
Up shadowy long-forgotten bowers

Of sculptured ivy and stone flowers—
Up many and many a marvellous shrine
Whose wreathéd friezes intertwine
The viol, the violet, and the vine.

Resignedly beneath the sky
The melancholy waters lie.
So blend the turrets and shadows there
That all seem pendulous in air,
While from a proud tower in the town
Death looks gigantically down.

Excerpt from "The City in the Sea," *Poems*

FAMILY

In February 1831, at the age of 22, Poe had a third book of poetry published, this one called simply *Poems*. Although the volume included several poems that were to become some of his best-known works—including "To Helen," "The City in the Sea," and "Israfel"—the book, like his previous two, received scant attention. His disappointment compounded growing health problems. He had begun fighting depression, and the opium he took to treat it gave him intense nightmares.

Poe soon went to Baltimore and found much-needed emotional support by moving in with members of his real father's family, including his grandmother; a kind aunt named Maria Clemm; Maria's young daughter Virginia; and his own brother, Henry. Sadly, Henry succumbed to tuberculosis and alcoholism shortly after Poe moved in. His death deprived Poe of all immediate family, as his sister, Rosalie, had lost her mind years before.

Once settled, Poe searched unsuccessfully for work as a teacher or newspaper reporter. He continued to write to John Allan on occasion to beg for money, as his relatives survived on only a small pension. In October 1831, he wrote a final letter to John, noting, "I am sorry that it is so seldom that I hear from you or even of you—for all communication seems to be at an end; and when I think of the long twenty-one years that I have called you father, and you have called me son, I could cry like a child to think that it should all end in this." When John died three years later, his foster son received not a cent of inheritance.

During the whole of a dull, dark, and soundless day in the autumn of the year, when the clouds hung oppressively low in the heavens, I had been passing alone, on horseback, through a singularly dreary tract of country; and at length found myself, as the shades of the evening drew on, within view of the melancholy House of Usher. I know not how it was—but, with the first glimpse of the building, a sense of insufferable gloom pervaded my spirit. I say insufferable; for the feeling was unrelieved by any of that half-pleasurable, because poetic, sentiment, with which the mind usually receives even the sternest natural images of the desolate or terrible. I looked upon the scene before me—upon the mere house, and the simple landscape features of the domain—upon the bleak walls—upon the vacant eye-like windows—upon a few rank sedges—and upon a few white trunks of decayed trees—with an utter depression of soul which I can compare to no earthly sensation more properly than to the after-dream of the reveller upon opium—the bitter lapse into everyday life—the hideous dropping off of the veil. There was an iciness, a sinking, a sickening of the heart—an unredeemed dreariness of thought which no goading of the imagination could torture into aught of the sublime. What was it—I paused to think—what was it that so unnerved me in the contemplation of the House of Usher? It was a mystery all insoluble; nor could I grapple with the shadowy fancies that crowded upon me as I pondered.

Excerpt from "The Fall of the House of Usher," *Tales*

Hollyer

Edgar Allan Poe, poet, author, and critic

Henry Wadsworth Longfellow (1807–1882)

James Fenimore Cooper (1789–1851)

Disheartened by the lack of attention his poems had received, Poe began writing short stories instead. In 1832, he had five stories published in the Philadelphia *Saturday Courier;* a year later, he won a much-needed $50 prize in a writing contest with his ghost-ship story "MS. Found in a Bottle." By the age of 24, Poe was the published author of numerous poems and tales and stood on the brink of literary success.

Yet as the young writer tried to entrench himself in America's literary establishment, something always disrupted him, sending him adrift. Over the course of the next decade, Poe would move from one East Coast city to another and from one editorial job to the next. Despite his better judgment, he seemed unable to stop himself from feuding with his bosses and embarking on drinking sprees that hurt his health and reputation.

Poe also did little to make friends among his colleagues. He worked as a literary critic during these years for such journals as Richmond's *Southern Literary Messenger.* Although he also penned stories and poems for the magazines, it was his scathing and arrogant reviews that earned him his first measure of fame. He frequently belittled the work of such popular literary figures as poet Henry Wadsworth Longfellow and novelist James Fenimore Cooper, and although readers enjoyed his brutal honesty, writers and fellow critics never forgot his attacks.

As Poe struggled to put down literary roots and continued waging his escalating battle against depression, loneliness, and drugs, he found a beacon of hope in his cousin Virginia. In May 1836, the two were married; Poe was 27, and Virginia was 13. Some scholars believe Poe married Virginia mostly to keep his aunt Maria, a motherly figure whom he adored, close to him. Regardless, the marriage was a happy one. Virginia's gentle nature gave Poe a safe harbor from his increasing mental anguish, and for the first time in his life, he had a real family of his own.

HYMN

*A*t morn—at noon—at twilight dim—

Maria! thou hast heard my hymn!

In joy and wo—in good and ill—

Mother of God, be with me still!

When the Hours flew brightly by,

And not a cloud obscured the sky,

My soul, lest it should truant be,

Thy grace did guide to thine and thee;

Now, when storms of Fate o'ercast

Darkly my Present and my Past,

Let my Future radiant shine

With sweet hopes of thee and thine!

From *The Raven and Other Poems*

DARKNESS

Poe's new family gave him some stability as he continued writing and moving from job to job during the late 1830s and early '40s. In late 1839, he published a two-volume collection entitled *Tales of the Grotesque and Arabesque*, which included the haunting "The Fall of the House of Usher" and every other short story he had written. The ground-breaking detective story "The Murders in the Rue Morgue" followed a year later. Despite the wild originality of his tales, they received little attention from critics or the public.

One cold January day in 1842, Poe, Virginia, and Maria were preparing to entertain guests in their modest but handsome Philadelphia home when Virginia coughed up blood—a tell-tale sign of tuberculosis. The critical calm of Poe's domestic existence was shattered. To escape from the overwhelming fear that stalked him, he wrote and drank like a madman. "I took leave of her forever and underwent all the agonies of her death," he later wrote of his young wife. "She recovered partially and again I hoped. At the end of a year the vessel broke again…. Then again—again—again and even once again…. I became insane, with long intervals of horrible sanity."

A painting believed to portray Virginia Poe

Poe channeled this torment into some of his finest—and darkest—work. In the year after Virginia's illness was revealed, Poe published "The Tell-Tale Heart," a chilling story of murder and insanity, and "The Pit and the Pendulum," the tale of a prisoner of war facing slow death under a huge, swinging blade. A third popular story, "The Gold Bug," conveyed Poe's fascination with cryptology, or the making and breaking of codes.

In April 1844, Poe and his family moved to New York City, where he found work as an assistant editor for the *Evening Mirror*. A year later, the magazine published a poem that at last made Poe famous: "The Raven." The poem tells of a man who—shut away on a desolate night, mourning the death of the woman he loved—is visited by a raven that knows only one word: "Nevermore." Readers in both America and Europe were entranced by the poem's dark beauty and hypnotic rhythm. For a while, the 36-year-old writer capitalized on its success by traveling from city to city to perform dramatic readings in dimly lit rooms.

Poe tried to use "The Raven" as a springboard to achieve his longstanding goal of owning his own literary magazine. In October 1845, he bought out the struggling *Broadway Journal* for $50, but his pet publication folded after just three months due to low readership. He was further distressed by the fact that although he had just published three more books, he still made barely enough money to support his family. Exhausted and overwhelmed with anxiety, he fell ill and could not work for months.

Once upon a midnight dreary, while I pondered, weak and weary,

Over many a quaint and curious volume of forgotten lore—

While I nodded, nearly napping, suddenly there came a tapping,

As of some one gently rapping, rapping at my chamber door.

"'Tis some visiter," I muttered, "tapping at my chamber door—

      Only this and nothing more."

Ah, distinctly I remember it was in the bleak December;

And each separate dying ember wrought its ghost upon the floor.

Eagerly I wished the morrow;—vainly I had sought to borrow

From my books surcease of sorrow—sorrow for the lost Lenore—

For the rare and radiant maiden whom the angels name Lenore—

      Nameless *here* for evermore.

And the silken, sad, uncertain rustling of each purple curtain

Thrilled me—filled me with fantastic terrors never felt before;

So that now, to still the beating of my heart, I stood repeating

"'Tis some visiter entreating entrance at my chamber door—

Some late visiter entreating entrance at my chamber door;—

      This it is and nothing more."

Presently my soul grew stronger; hesitating then no longer,

"Sir," said I, "or Madam, truly your forgiveness I implore;

But the fact is I was napping, and so gently you came rapping,

And so faintly you came tapping, tapping at my chamber door,

That I scarce was sure I heard you"—here I opened wide the door;—

      Darkness there and nothing more.

Deep into that darkness peering, long I stood there wondering, fearing,

Doubting, dreaming dreams no mortal ever dared to dream before;

But the silence was unbroken, and the stillness gave no token,

And the only word there spoken was the whispered word, "Lenore?"

This I whispered, and an echo murmured back the word, "Lenore!"

      Merely this and nothing more.

Back into the chamber turning, all my soul within me burning,

Soon again I heard a tapping somewhat louder than before.

"Surely," said I, "surely that is something at my window lattice;

Let me see, then, what thereat is, and this mystery explore—

Let my heart be still a moment and this mystery explore;—

      'Tis the wind and nothing more!"

Open here I flung the shutter, when, with many a flirt and flutter,

In there stepped a stately Raven of the saintly days of yore;

Not the least obeisance made he; not a minute stopped or stayed he;

But, with mien of lord or lady, perched above my chamber door—

Perched upon a bust of Pallas just above my chamber door—

      Perched, and sat, and nothing more.

Then this ebony bird beguiling my sad fancy into smiling,

By the grave and stern decorum of the countenance it wore,

"Though thy crest be shorn and shaven, thou," I said, "art sure no craven,

Ghastly grim and ancient Raven wandering from the Nightly shore—

Tell me what thy lordly name is on the Night's Plutonian shore!"

      Quoth the Raven "Nevermore."

Excerpt from "The Raven," *The Raven and Other Poems*

UNIQUELY POE

*A*s Poe grew older, his poems and tales became increasingly dark, full of shadows and imagined demons, and ringing with themes of sadness, fear, and longing. He thought that the purpose of writing was to "amuse by arousing thought," and many of his works were characterized by intense sensory description. He believed that poems derived much of their emotional impact from the "sweet sound" of their rhyme, and he developed a versification, or style of poetic music, that pulled the reader forward with lulling but inescapable rhythms.

With rare exceptions, most of Poe's poems and tales were ignored upon publication or dismissed as immoral drivel. There were unspoken rules to writing in America in the early 1800s. Literature was to be instructive, focused on the community, and set in America. Poe took a different path. In sharp contrast to these wholesome guidelines, he penned poems and stories that were sad or horrific, often focused on isolated individuals in Gothic, or Medieval-like, settings.

For his rebellion against the literary norm, Poe and his work were widely labeled simple-minded, vulgar, and un-American. The poet Ralph Waldo Emerson famously dismissed him as "the jingle man," a slap at the sing-song poetic rhythms Poe favored. Although much of the reading public saw him as pompous, such criticism wounded his sensitive pride. Poe's genius would never truly be appreciated during his lifetime. Even after his death, it would be the French—not his fellow Americans—who would first embrace the forlorn beauty of his words.

2

*H*ear the mellow wedding bells—

Golden bells!

What a world of happiness their harmony foretells!

Through the balmy air of night

How they ring out their delight!—

From the molten-golden notes

And all in tune,

What a liquid ditty floats

To the turtle-dove that listens while she gloats

On the moon!

Oh, from out the sounding cells

What a gush of euphony voluminously wells!

How it swells!

How it dwells

On the Future!—how it tells

Of the rapture that impels

To the swinging and the ringing

Of the bells, bells, bells!—

Of the bells, bells, bells, bells,

Bells, bells, bells—

To the rhyming and the chiming of the bells!

3

Hear the loud alarum bells—

Brazen bells!

What tale of terror, now, their turbulency tells!

In the startled ear of Night

How they scream out their affright!

Too much horrified to speak,

They can only shriek, shriek,

Out of tune,

In a clamorous appealing to the mercy of the fire—

In a mad expostulation with the deaf and frantic fire,

Leaping higher, higher, higher,

With a desperate desire

And a resolute endeavor

Now—now to sit, or never,

By the side of the pale-faced moon.

Oh, the bells, bells, bells!

What a tale their terror tells

Of despair!

How they clang and clash and roar!

What a horror they outpour

In the bosom of the palpitating air!

Yet the ear, it fully knows,

By the twanging

And the clanging,

How the danger ebbs and flows:—

Yes, the ear distinctly tells,

In the jangling

And the wrangling,

How the danger sinks and swells,

By the sinking or the swelling in the anger of the bells—

Of the bells—

Of the bells, bells, bells, bells,

Bells, bells, bells—

In the clamor and the clangor of the bells.

Excerpt from "The Bells," *Collected Works of Edgar Allan Poe*

THE CLIFF

On January 30, 1847, just a few months after Poe's family moved to a small country cottage in Fordham, New York, Virginia died at the age of 24. Although her death was long in coming, it left Poe a hollow man. For weeks, he would wander outside in the middle of the night to weep over her grave.

Little by little, Poe returned to his writing, his pet cat perched across his shoulders. He had returned to poetry and spent this time turning out such works as the strangely philosophical prose poem "Eureka" and the raging "The Bells." Yet despite Poe's efforts to return to normalcy, Virginia's death had broken him, and his health and psyche would never be sound again. "He did not seem to care, after she was gone, whether he lived an hour, a day, a week, or a year," one acquaintance noted.

In early 1848, Poe embarked on a tour of public readings. He often used the opportunities in front of crowds to defend his character, in particular his notorious problems with drugs. "I have absolutely no pleasure in the stimulants in which I sometimes so madly indulge," he said. "It has not been in pursuit of pleasure that I have periled life and reputation and reason. It has been in the desperate attempt to escape from torturing memories, from a sense of insupportable loneliness, and a dread of some strange and impending doom."

Poe's lonely cottage in Fordham, New York

We walk about, amid the destinies of our world-existence, encompassed by dim but ever present *Memories* of a Destiny more vast—very distant in the by-gone time, and infinitely awful.

We live out a Youth peculiarly haunted by such shadows; yet never mistaking them for dreams. As Memories we *know* them. *During our Youth* the distinction is too clear to deceive us even for a moment.

So long as this Youth endures, the feeling *that we exist*, is the most natural of all feelings. We understand it *thoroughly*. That there was a period at which we did *not* exist—or, that it might so have happened that we never had existed at all—are the considerations, indeed, which *during this Youth*, we find difficulty in understanding. Why we should *not* exist, is, *up to the epoch of our Manhood*, of all queries the most unanswerable. Existence—self-existence—existence from all Time and to all Eternity—seems, up to the epoch of Manhood, a normal and unquestionable condition:—*seems, because it is*.

But now comes the period at which a conventional World-Reason awakens us from the truth of our dream. Doubt, Surprise and Incomprehensibility arrive at the same moment. They say:—"You live and the time was when you lived not. You have been created. An Intelligence exists greater than your own; and it is only through this Intelligence you live at all." These things we struggle to comprehend and cannot:—*cannot*, because these things, being untrue, are thus, of necessity, incomprehensible.

Excerpt from "Eureka"

*E*ven as he defended his reputation, Poe's behavior grew increasingly strange in 1848 and 1849. During his travels, he often went on drinking binges and issued dueling challenges to other writers and editors. On one trip through Philadelphia, he became convinced that two men were trying to kill him and fled the train, hiding at a friend's house for two weeks. Still, he managed to pen "Annabel Lee" during this time, a ballad that would garner lasting popularity.

Poe engaged in a series of bizarre flirtations during this period, writing love letters to many women, some of them married. On one trip to Richmond in mid-1849, he met his boyhood sweetheart, Elmira Royster, now widowed, and begged her to marry him. The two seemed to have reached a verbal agreement of sorts when Poe departed, promising to return promptly. He never would.

On October 3, after going missing for several days, Poe was found in a gutter outside a Baltimore tavern, unconscious, filthy, and dressed in strange clothes. How he arrived there remains a mystery, although theories of foul play, alcohol poisoning, and rabies have all been proffered. He regained consciousness the next day in Washington Hospital but was incoherent, trembling and ranting. After a period of violent deliriousness in which he seemed to fight against ghosts, Poe at last grew calm with exhaustion. On October 7, America's misfit poet cried weakly, "Lord, help my poor soul!" and died. He was 40 years old.

Two and a half decades later, the poet Walt Whitman told of a dream he had of a battered ship caught in a raging storm in the dead of night. "On the deck was a slender, slight, beautiful figure, a dim man, apparently enjoying all the terror, the murk, and the dislocation of which he was the center and the victim. That figure of my lurid dream might stand for Edgar Poe, his spirit, his fortunes, and his poems—themselves all lurid dreams."

ANNABEL LEE

*I*t was many and many a year ago,
 In a kingdom by the sea,
That a maiden there lived whom you may know
 By the name of Annabel Lee;—
And this maiden she lived with no other thought
 Than to love and be loved by me.

She was a child and *I* was a child,
 In this kingdom by the sea,
But we loved with a love that was more than love—
 I and my Annabel Lee—
With a love that the wingéd seraphs of Heaven
 Coveted her and me.

And this was the reason that, long ago,
 In this kingdom by the sea,
A wind blew out of a cloud by night
 Chilling my Annabel Lee;
So that her high-born kinsmen came
 And bore her away from me,
To shut her up in a sepulchre
 In this kingdom by the sea.

The angels, not half so happy in Heaven,
 Went envying her and me;
Yes! that was the reason (as all men know,
 In this kingdom by the sea)
That the wind came out of the cloud, chilling
 And killing my Annabel Lee.

But our love it was stronger by far than the love
 Of those who were older than we—
 Of many far wiser than we—
And neither the angels in Heaven above
 Nor the demons down under the sea
Can ever dissever my soul from the soul
 Of the beautiful Annabel Lee:—

For the moon never beams without bringing me dreams
 Of the beautiful Annabel Lee;
And the stars never rise but I see the bright eyes
 Of the beautiful Annabel Lee;
And so, all the night-tide, I lie down by the side
Of my darling, my darling, my life and my bride
 In her sepulchre there by the sea—
 In her tomb by the side of the sea.

From *The Works of the Late Edgar Allan Poe*

ACKNOWLEDGMENTS

PHOTO CREDITS

Photographs by Corbis (Bettmann, Photo Collection Alexander Alland, Sr., Stapleton Collection), Getty Images (Hulton Archive, Rischgitz)

Photographs on pages 12–13, 17, 23, 32–33, 36, 37, 42–43, and 48 by Tina Mucci. Copyright © 1993 Tina Mucci. First published in *Poe* by Creative Editions 1993.

ILLUSTRATION CREDITS

Illustrations on cover and pages 1, 3, 4–5, 7, 10–11, 15, 18–19, 22, 24, 28–29, 34–35, 38, 41, and 45 by Gary Kelley. Copyright © 2006 Gary Kelley.

SELECTED WORKS BY EDGAR ALLAN POE

POETRY
Tamerlane and Other Poems, 1827
Al Aaraaf, Tamerlane and Minor Poems, 1829
Poems, 1831
The Raven and Other Poems, 1845
Eureka, 1848

PROSE
The Narrative of Arthur Gordon Pym, 1838
Tales of the Grotesque and Arabesque, 1839
The Prose Romances of Edgar A. Poe, 1843
Tales, 1845

NOTABLE POSTHUMOUS WORKS
The Works of the Late Edgar Allan Poe, 1850–1856
Prose Tales, 1898
The Complete Works of Edgar Allan Poe, 1902
Collected Works of Edgar Allan Poe, 1969

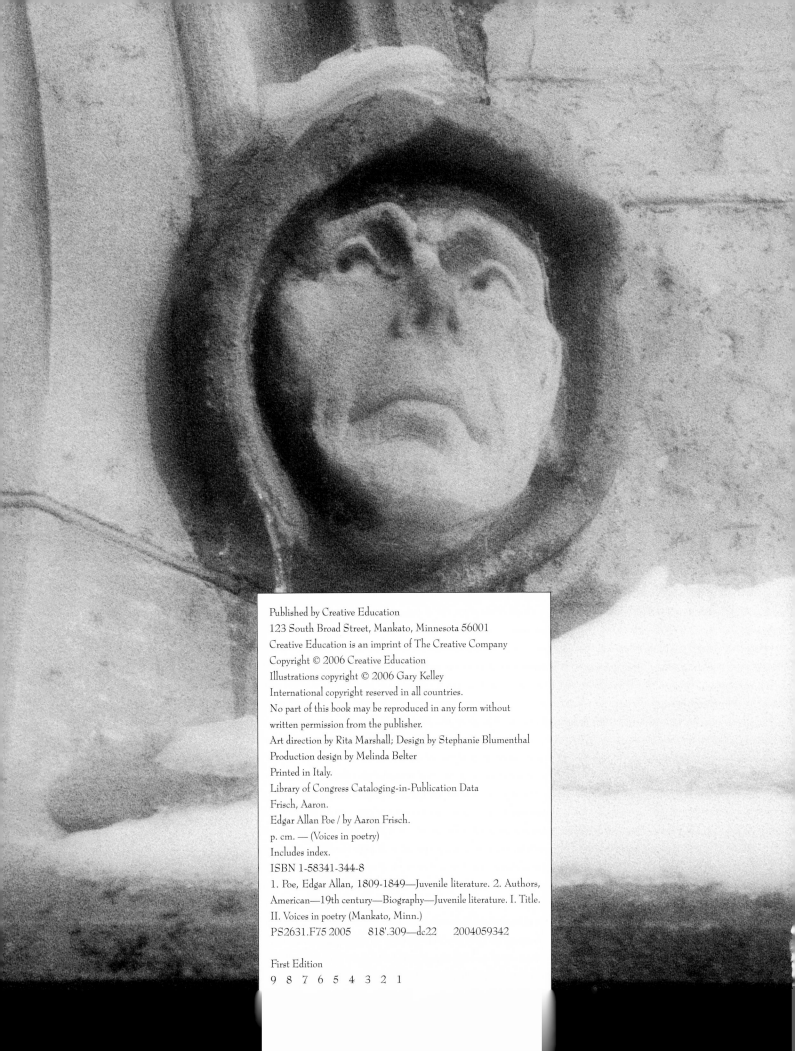

Published by Creative Education

123 South Broad Street, Mankato, Minnesota 56001

Creative Education is an imprint of The Creative Company

Copyright © 2006 Creative Education

Illustrations copyright © 2006 Gary Kelley

International copyright reserved in all countries.

Art direction by Rita Marshall; Design by Stephanie Blumenthal

Production design by Melinda Belter

Printed in Italy.

Library of Congress Cataloging-in-Publication Data

Frisch, Aaron.

Edgar Allan Poe / by Aaron Frisch.

p. cm. — (Voices in poetry)

Includes index.

ISBN 1-58341-344-8

1. Poe, Edgar Allan, 1809-1849—Juvenile literature. 2. Authors,
American—19th century—Biography—Juvenile literature. I. Title.
II. Voices in poetry (Mankato, Minn.)

PS2631.F75 2005   818'.309—dc22   2004059342

First Edition

9 8 7 6 5 4 3 2 1